The former Hillburn School, which now serves as the
headquarters for the Ramapo Central School District.
(2014) Photographer: Mary Galindez Short.

To Candice —
Keep fighting the good fight!

IT TAKES A VILLAGE

The Integration of the Hillburn School System

Leonard M. Alexander "Pete"
Leonard M. Alexander
with Peter C. Alexander

PAGE PUBLISHING, INC.
New York, NY

First originally published by Page Publishing, Inc. 2014

ISBN 978-1-63417-331-5 (pbk)
ISBN 978-1-63417-332-2 (digital)

Printed in the United States of America

Cover image: The former Hillburn School, which now serves as the headquarters for the Ramapo Central School District. (2014) Photographer: Mary Galindez Short.

———∿∿∘ᑲᏩᏩᏕᏩᑲᎧᏩᎧᎧ∿∿———

To the matriarch of our family, Muriel E. Alexander,
an exceptional wife, mother, and grandmother.

———∿∿∘ᑲᏩᏩᏕᏩᑲᎧᏩᎧᎧ∿∿———

ACKNOWLEDGMENTS

We are especially grateful to Muriel Alexander for reading earlier versions of this book and to Paducah, Kentucky, attorney R. Brent Vasseur for giving the manuscript a fresh set of eyes.

We also thank the Rockland County (New York) Commission on Human Rights for honoring the civil rights contributions of our patriarch, Thomas Ulysses Alexander, and for making available to us the correspondence between him, the NAACP, and the New York State Education Department; access to that information was invaluable.

INTRODUCTION

Everyone has studied the twentieth century struggle to integrate the public schools in the United States and to move the civil rights agenda forward. The United States Supreme Court's historic decision in the *Brown v. Board of Education* case changed the course of events for families of color forever because separate schools, divided by race, were declared to be unconstitutional. After *Brown*, white schools were no longer just for white students.

Most people believe that the problem of segregated schools was unique to the southern states, but that belief would be incorrect. Segregation existed throughout the United States, and school systems that were separated by race were often as easy to find north of the Mason-Dixon line as they were south of the Mason-Dixon line.

I am a mixed-race, brown-skinned man who was born and raised in suburban New York City. For most of my life I was considered either colored or Negro. In fact, my heritage is quite diverse. My ancestors are African, Dutch, and Native American. I'm sure that I have other ethnic roots, but I'm still discovering them. For purposes of attending elementary school, however, I was just one of the colored kids, and colored kids in Hillburn, New York, had to attend the colored school.

This book is the story of one of those segregated northern schools. It is my story, told with the help of my oldest son so that a more complete history of race in our country may be recorded for future generations.

CHAPTER 1

HILLBURN, NEW YORK

Just forty miles northwest of New York City lies a sleepy little village called Hillburn, New York. It is the first community on the busy Route 17 state highway as you enter New York State from New Jersey on your way to the Catskill Mountains. Throughout most of the twentieth century, Route 17 was the preferred four-lane highway that city dwellers and suburbanites used to escape Manhattan and its surroundings. The Catskills were home to entertainment venues that featured headline acts such as Henny Youngman, Sammy Davis Jr., and Jerry Lewis. The region was more commonly known as the Borscht Belt or the Jewish Alps, and entertainers would welcome the opportunity to perform for the many fans who spent summers and weekends year-round in Upstate New York.

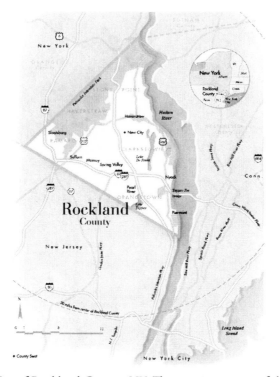

Map of Rockland County, NY. The map is courtesy of the
Rockland Economic Development Corporation.

Hillburn is located in a valley among the Ramapo Mountains, and it is part of the township of Ramapo. *Ramapo* refers to my Native American ancestors who settled the valley. They were called Ramapoughs, which is thought to mean either "sweet water" or "sloping/slanting rocks." Hillburn is a small village of 2.2 square miles located in the Ramapo Pass, a part of the lower Hudson Valley, and it is bisected by Route 17 slightly toward the western edge of town and bordered by the Ramapo River and the Erie Railroad Tracks (now New Jersey Transit) and the New York State Thruway to the northeast. Hillburn's population is just shy of 1,000 people, about the same as where its population has been for decades. It has always been a quiet place. The village has no shopping centers or supermarkets; people travel to nearby Suffern, New York, or Mahwah or Ramsey, New Jersey, for those amenities. It has no tourist destinations or famous historical sites, save for a Revolutionary War marker along Route 17 and a special plaque in front of the Hillburn school. The Revolutionary War marker commemorates the advance of General George Washington's troops through Hillburn on the way to a battle in Maryland, and the plaque in front of Hillburn School memorializes another war—the war waged to integrate the village's school system.

Route 17 is noteworthy for another reason. It divided the village along racial lines for the most part. All of the white families lived between the highway and the Ramapo River, and nearly all of the colored families lived on the other side of the highway. Racial identity is a complicated concept, but *colored* was the most common way in which my people were categorized through most of my life. For purposes of this narrative, I choose to continue to refer to my people as colored as a way to maintain historical accuracy.

Street map of Hillburn, New York (2014) © OpenStreetMap contributors. The data is available under the Open Database License and the cartography is licensed as CC BY-SA.

Hillburn was chartered in 1893. It was originally known as Woodburn. According to David Cole, author of *The History of Rockland County*, the original name was likely chosen because the village was surrounded by woods and was near to water.[1] *Burn* is Scottish for *stream*, which may have been a reference to the Ramapo River that runs alongside of the village. The year before the village was established, an application to the US Post Office revealed that there was another community in New York called Woodburn. As a result, the original name was scrapped, and Hillburn was the name selected.[2]

The prominent families in town were named Suffern, Davidson, Banker, Pierson, Snow, and Creelman. The Sufferns were the same family for whom nearby Suffern, New York, was named. Suffern is a larger village, filled with shops and businesses, and it is where Hillburn children attended high school. It is the birthplace of actors Tyne Daly and David Annable and former NFL linebacker Keith Bulluck. I don't recall exactly how the Suffern family made its money, but the popular talk around Hillburn was they were given land grants from England and had capitalized on those investments. J. Edgar Davidson owned significant land on the east side of Hillburn and was best known as a philanthropist. Charlie Banker was a decent fellow, but I don't know where he was from or how he made his living. He served as the mayor of Hillburn for a relatively short stretch. The Piersons were a wealthy family from England; much of their money was earned from the manufacture of nails, wire, and smelting metal. The Snows were landholders and owned much of the land on top of one of the mountains that surrounds Hillburn. They had a turkey farm and raised cattle. John Creelman was the president (mayor) of Hillburn for over forty years.[3] He was a powerful man, born in Nova Scotia, and served as mayor even though many Hillburn residents believed that he was not a citizen of the United States. Most of these founding families were white immigrants from England or Canada; all were influential in one way or another.

The history of Hillburn cannot be written without including stories about John Suffern, the patriarch of the Suffern clan. He provided the land that became Hillburn. Suffern was a very powerful man. He was a northern Irishman from County Antrim.[4] His ancestors were from France. Among his many pursuits, he owned a tavern in Suffern,

New York. On July 19, 1777, then-general George Washington was a guest of his establishment.[5] From that location, Washington wrote a letter to congress to recommend that Robert Erskine be commissioned to assist our young nation. Erskine was from nearby northern New Jersey, and among his many other accomplishments, he drafted 129 military maps that marked the chief roads and homes that existed in New York and New Jersey. My wife's relatives, specifically her father's brother-in-law, our uncle Everett, was one of many illegitimate, mixed-race offspring of the Suffern family.

Suffern was a man who accomplished much during his life. He started a grist mill, a forge, a woolen factory, a sawmill, a potash works, a store, ironworks, and many other endeavors. He organized the First Reformed Church in neighboring Mahwah, New Jersey; he was the first postmaster in Rockland County (the county in which Hillburn is located); and he served as a state senator.[6] Suffern died in 1836 at age ninety-five. He had three sons, all of whom were equally prominent in their respective business and political pursuits.[7]

In 1795, Suffern sold 119 acres of land to brothers Josiah, Jeremiah, and Isaac Pierson.[8] That land was settled as the community of Ramapo, a name that paid tribute to the Ramapough Mountain Indians, the Native Americans who settled along the border of New York and New Jersey. Ramapo is an unincorporated area located adjacent to Hillburn, and it is also the name of the township that surrounds the village of Hillburn.

John Creelman was not only the longtime mayor, but he was also instrumental in helping a group of Hillburn citizens establish the village's first fire department in 1894. The men who organized the department selected another prominent resident, F. W. Snow, as the first chief. The man whom I recall as his brother, William. W. Snow, provided a facility in which the new fire department could hold meetings and store equipment. William Snow was the general manager of the Ramapo Wheel and Foundry Co., and he and his wife donated land and money to build the first firehouse.[9]

The Piersons lived in the village of Sloatsburg, which was about seven miles northwest of Hillburn, and they owned the Ramapough Iron Works. The ironworks operated in a plant of considerable size between Hillburn and Sloatsburg, and it employed many of the colored men and women from Ringwood, New Jersey, which was a village just over the state border from Hillburn. If you didn't work for the Piersons, you worked for Mr. Davidson; that's all the work there was for my people.

J. Edgar Davidson is, perhaps, the most pivotal player in the history of the struggle for civil rights in Hillburn. He was regarded by nearly everyone as a pillar of the community. He was a 1908 graduate of Cornell University.[10] He was vice president of the Ramapough Iron Works plant near Hillburn, and he was the chairman of the Hillburn School Board of Education, and he was the chairman of the local savings and loan in Suffern. The Ramapo Iron Works was created by Jeremiah Pierson, another important Hillburn citizen, and the company was responsible for producing cut nails, wood screws, cotton cloth, and spring steel. It was a thriving company and was the place of employment for many of Hillburn's colored residents. Davidson was what we might now think of as the COO of the business.

Mr. Davidson was generally known around town for his charity, but a lot of us didn't think his motivations were entirely pure. I thought that he was always positioning himself to make sure that the colored people in Hillburn had to rely on him for nearly everything. As a result of his activities, Mr. Davidson was treated like royalty in Hillburn. Each year, Brook Church, the colored church, held a Thanksgiving dinner for the community, and it was always well attended. People were always in a very jovial mood, but when the Davidsons would arrive, people immediately quieted down, and the Davidsons would cut in line and were served immediately. I always noticed that they would always bring their own plates and silverware. Even though they did appear at the colored church to dine with the colored residents, they would not eat off of our plates or use our utensils.

As impressive as he certainly was, J. Edgar Davidson was also somewhat of a mysterious figure in Hillburn. He wasn't seen around the village very often, except at school board meetings. He would make occasional appearances to my side of the village, however, just before each municipal election. He would drive his big Chrysler Imperial over to the colored section of town and would hand out candy to the children. He would ask each kid what his or her name was and what their fathers did for a living. As long as the surname wasn't Alexander, they would get candy. I recall that he was not shy about denying candy to my siblings and me. On each election day, he would again drive to the homes of certain families in the colored section and give them rides to the polling station. Many of the colored residents had very little in the way of material things, so Mr. Davidson's largesse was a welcome gift and would ensure that Mr. Davidson's people would remain in power.

Siblings Mildred Alexander Galindez, age 6 and Leonard "Pete" Alexander, age 5. There were seven Alexander children, one girl and six boys. As a result, Mildred was known simply as "Sis" her entire life. [Photo courtesy of Leonard Alexander]

From left to right: Thomas Edward "Eddie" Alexander, Charles Francis "Frank" Alexander, Theodore Walker, and Eddie Robinson (circa 1943) [Photo courtesy of Leonard Alexander]

Mr. Davidson's daughter, Jean Davidson, grew up in Hillburn, and despite growing up in privilege, she was remarkably down-to-earth. Over her lifetime, she enjoyed professional achievements as an attorney and, later, a judge. After her parents died, Judge Davidson was noticeably friendly to most people, and she was regarded as a generous contributor to the Hillburn community. She went out of her way to help several of the colored Hillburn residents obtain jobs in the Rockland County post offices, which had been segregated for many years. Also, my sons often joined other Hillburn children to go sledding on her estate each winter.

Among my relatives, there were also noteworthy historical figures. My ancestors, the DeFreeses and the DeGroats, settled in Rockland County from Orange County in the mid-1800s. Orange was the county immediately to the northwest of Rockland. My people were referred to as mulatto because they were a mixed-race people. They were a combination of European whites, Negro, and Native American. The US Census listed them as being mulatto, so the term was used to describe them for years. When they came to Hillburn, these people lived along the mountains that bordered Hillburn to the southeast. They were respected as being honest, hardworking, and nonviolent people.

Most of my ancestors worked at the Hillburn rail yard. Sam DeFreese Sr., my great-grandfather, was the foreman of those who worked out in the rail yard. His sons and their sons made up much of the workforce. Sam Sr. was known as a preacher, and with the help of John DeGroat and Elliot Mann, he asked some of the mountain property owners for land and for permission the take enough wood to build a place in which to worship. My great-grandfather and his colleagues were granted that permission. Before receiving permission, my ancestors had what were called cabin meetings. In 1877, Messrs. DeFreese, DeGroat, and Mann, among others, built what was called the mountain chapel, also called Brook Chapel. Sam Sr. became the preacher. Sam Jr.'s wife became the organist. She not only played the organ, she also taught many of the colored people to play the piano.

Samuel E. DeFreese, Sr. (circa 1870) [Photo courtesy of Leonard Alexander]

In the late 1800s, many other mixed-race people arrived in Hillburn. Some people came from western New Jersey, and many others came from Maryland and Virginia. There weren't enough places to live so the homes were built further up the mountainside on what is Boulder Avenue today. They were built specifically for the men who worked at the Hillburn rail yard. Those men, who were all classed as being Negro, married many of the women of the DeFreese and DeGroat families, which mixed up the races a bit more. Men with surnames of Duncan and Farmer came from Virginia, and men named Morton, Boddy, Watkins, and, I believe, Jackson, all found their way to Hillburn from Maryland. I specifically remember that Mr. Morton was J. Edgar Davidson's chauffer, and he always had a very nice car. I don't know how Mr. Morton earned enough money to have nice cars, but he always did. He was known in our neighborhood as the King Fish. Mr. Farmer's and Mr. Morton's homes had bathrooms inside the houses. Not very many of the other colored family homes had inside bathrooms. The houses built up on Boulder Avenue also had inside bathrooms and, eventually, so did the house in which the Brook Chapel minister lived.

The men who moved here from Maryland and Virginia and who married the local women all found housing in town. I have no idea as to how they found a place to live and somehow they were all able to *own* their homes. That was almost impossible considering the little bit of money they were paid for the work they did. At times, when they weren't working, they received assistance from the county. Similarly, in the early 1900s, my mother, Sara DeFreese, went to Howard University. I don't know how she could afford to go there. I believe that, somehow, her education was supposed to prepare her to teach in the segregated school system; although she never did teach in a Hillburn school.

Before my mother graduated from Howard, she married Thomas Ulysses Alexander, a man who had been born and raised in the Washington, DC, area. To my siblings and me, he was "Pop," and when he learned of the segregated schools in Hillburn, Pop began to see if he could help eliminate the discrimination. When the local school board authorities found out that he was working to oppose the segregation, they chose Mildred Van Dunk and Hulda DeFreese, other mixed-race Hillburn residents, to replace my mother as school teacher in the colored school. It is my belief that Mr. Davidson was the person who provided the financing for all of the ladies from Hillburn to go to Howard University. I also believe that my father's denunciation of the segregated school system to be the reason my mother never ever had the opportunity to teach in the Hillburn schools.

Thomas and Sara DeFreese Alexander with children Eddie, Frank, and Billy. (circa 1925) [Photo courtesy of Leonard Alexander]

CHAPTER 2

THE STRUGGLE FOR EQUALITY

Hillburn, New York, has always been a simple, quiet community. Part of its charm was the appearance that people of different races lived in harmony. The harmony, unfortunately, was attributable only to the social norms of the time. The white men in the village controlled every-thing—jobs, banks, land. and the colored people, as we were known and referred to, would be taken care of as long as we stayed in our place.

"Our place" meant we should not be too vocal or too uppity. Also, "our place" meant that we would live on the colored side of town (with the dividing line being Route 17). "Our place" also meant that we would attend a separate school from the main grammar school in the village. Since 1889, four years before the village of Hillburn was chartered, the colored children attended grammar school that was set aside for us. The school was situated alongside a babbling brook and was known as Brook School. Unofficially, it was the colored school.

Brook School, also called the "colored school," Hillburn, NY (circa 1930). This image was taken from the Hillburn Centennial Yearbook and is made available courtesy of the Village of Hillburn Board, the Centennial Committee, and the Historical Society.

Hillburn schools were not the only segregated institutions in the village. In our small community of one thousand people, there were two Presbyterian churches. Ramapo Presbyterian Church was the white church, and Brook Presbyterian Church was the colored church.

Ramapo Presbyterian Church (2014).
Photographer: Mary Galindez Short

Brook Presbyterian Church (2014). This church is the successor to Brook Chapel. Photographer: Lisa Jennings

Brook Church began as Brook Chapel, a small structure built along a brook upstream from Brook School. My great-grandfather, Samuel DeFreese Sr., was the first preacher of Brook Chapel.

Brook Chapel, which existed from 1877 until 1893. (circa 1880) Children attending Sunday School or class are visible on the front porch. The church was constructed by founding pastor Samuel E. DeFreese, Sr. and John DeGroat among others. [Photo courtesy of Leonard Alexander]

Unlike communities in the south, there were no signs saying "White" and "Colored" in Hillburn, but everyone knew that certain places were off-limits to the coloreds. Our little village was not alone in the metropolitan New York City area. One day, our church went on a fieldtrip to Palisades Amusement Park, an entertainment venue in northern New Jersey. It was a Wednesday, which was known locally as Maid's Day-Off Day, so there were a lot of children at the park. My friends and I entered the park, and my shirttail cousin, Nick Van Dunk, and his brother attempted to go swimming in the park's pool. Nick was fairly light-skinned because of the years of intermarriage of African Americans, whites, and Ramapough Mountain Indians, and he entered the pool. When Nick's brother attempted to enter the pool, the Palisades Park authorities forbid him from entering the pool because he had a dark complexion. He explained that his brother was already in the pool. The employees asked him to point out his brother, and after he did, Nick was removed from the pool.

CHAPTER 3

THE NAACP

By 1930, the struggle to provide a better education for the colored children of Hillburn was on the front burner in our home. My father, Thomas Ulysses Alexander, was the president of the Hillburn chapter of the NAACP. He and my mother, Sara DeFreese Alexander, wanted to see the Hillburn school system integrated, but they needed help. My parents, particularly my father, doggedly pursued equality in a very quiet manner. In 1930, I was just two years old, but I'm pretty sure that none of my siblings really knew just how involved he was in the effort to end Jim Crow in our little northern village.

Leonard "Pete" Alexander cutting the hair of his father, Thomas Alexander. (circa 1945) [Photo courtesy of Leonard Alexander]

Many of Hillburn's other colored families thought of my father as a troublemaker because he would repeatedly question the white authorities about the disparate educational treatment of the colored children. In 1930, the school board voted to purchase a lot next to the white school to turn it into a playground. Pop questioned the board's authority to purchase the land and build recreation facilities without providing similar facilities at the colored school. His protest, twenty-four years before the supreme court's historic ruling in *Brown v. Board of Education*, gained no traction with J. Edgar Davidson and the board. However, Pop believed that the colored citizens of Hillburn were now finally ready to fight their separate and unequal treatment. He visited the New York City office of the NAACP and registered his complaints with the civil rights organization.

The NAACP had investigated the Hillburn school system years before, but nothing happened. After my father's visit, however, Special Legal Assistant William T. Andrews was assigned to the case. Mr. Andrews immediately contacted the New York State Education Department and began his investigation. He received word from the state education department that the public schools in New York were required to comply with section 40 of the Civil Rights Law as amended by Chapter 196 of the Laws of 1913.[11] Armed with this information, Mr. Andrews began his work in earnest.

Andrews learned from the state that there were 301 students registered in District 15 in the town of Ramapo (the Hillburn school system), but the state could not provide a breakdown of the student population by school. My father was able to supply Andrews with the missing information, and on September 6, 1930, Pop wrote that "there are 113 children of our group registered so far. They expect a few more."[12] "Our group" meant the colored children who attended the colored school, which was officially known as Brook School.

Postcard from Thomas Alexander to NAACP Special
Legal Assistant William T. Andrews. (1930)

Brook School was a simple structure, a wooden building that had two entrances. On the north side of the building was the entrance to the first, second, third, and fourth grades. On the south side was the entrance to the fifth, sixth, seventh, and eighth grades. Each entrance had a small cloakroom just inside the door, and the classrooms were simple and shared by multiple grades.

There wasn't much incentive to go to school, so many students quit when they reached sixteen years old. The only work in the area was at the Ramapo Iron Works or the Mahwah Iron Works. At the end of the day, the men who worked in those places came out of the buildings covered with soot. Conditions were so bad in those plants that you couldn't tell who was who or what race any of the individuals were because they were all covered in a thick, dark coating every day.

In early 1931, NAACP attorney Andrews visited Hillburn on a fact-finding mission and, in February, he reported his findings. After meeting with the principal, who was responsible for both schools, school board president J. Edgar Davidson, and one other board member, he wrote:

> It developed that there are four colored teachers
> and seven white teachers employed in the town for
> the two schools. These schools are Main school and
> Brook School.

The Main School is good looking and a fairly large brick building with good equipment. It has two stories and a basement; fairly ample ground outside for recreational purposes, including a tennis court and other outdoor facilities and it also has running water within the building for sanitary purposes. There are about 313 pupils in both schools, 115 being in the Brook School, divided into classes from the first to the eighth grades. There are also six Negro children in the kindergarten department. This department meets in the afternoon in the Main building. The same kindergarten teacher holds classes for white and colored pupils, but the white pupils' classes are in the morning.

We went over to the Brook School and inspected that. It is a little neat, nice-looking, four-room wooden structure. One room has some braces to support to strengthen one wall. These braces had been put up since the building was erected. Two classes are held by individual teachers, both in the same room. The building was clean, well heated, well lighted, and has running water for drinking purposes in the halls and one toilet for the teachers indoors. The pupils' toilet facilities has no running water and were about 25 feet removed from the building and made altogether a walk of about 150 or 200 feet from the steps to the little houses. They were clean but unlighted and unheated. For ventilation purposes, one window had been broken out and wooden bars placed across it. There was very little space for recreational purposes.[13]

Brook School, as seen from Rte. #17 in Hillburn, New York.
(circa 1950s) [Photo courtesy of Leonard Alexander]

Andrews also wrote that school board president Davidson, the other board member, and the principal tried to defend the separate schools. Mr. Davidson "contended that harmonious relationship between the two races in Hillburn were aided by the separate schools and the discontinuance of the policy would precipitate trouble."[14] Andrews also wrote that Davidson acknowledged that my father had a government job (with the US Post Office in Manhattan) and was not in fear of losing his job because of his civil rights activities. Andrews explained that "Hillburn…is supposed to be a manufacturing town, most of the manufactures being controlled, at one time at least, by the Davidson family. Mr. J. E. Davidson now being the business representative of the family's interest."[15]

Andrews was unable to meet any of the teachers from either school during his visit, but the principal of the white school told him that "within recent years all teachers are required to be at least a graduate from a normal school."[16] In addition to the information that Andrews learned from the school officials, he also learned from Pop that the quality of instruction at Brook School was subpar. Andrews wrote, "Mr. Alexander inferred that the Negro teachers were incompetent or at least not interested in their work."[17]

It is odd that Mr. Andrews would have attributed to my father a feeling that the Negro teachers were subpar. First, he would have no reason to know the caliber of the teachers. He did not attend the school, and my siblings and I did not come home from school and complain about them with any regularity. His perceived criticism might have had some merit, however.

During my years at Brook School, two of the teachers were brought to Hillburn from down south. One was Ethel Roseboro, who was from North Carolina and who taught the third and fourth grades. The other teacher, Kate Lord Savory, was from a family of teachers from Talladega, Alabama. The women lived with Miss Savory's two sisters, Cicely Gunner and a Mrs. Love. The male in the household was named Reverend Gunner. I don't know how he was related to Cicely, but I think she was his wife. He became the minister at Brook Chapel, our family's church just up the road from Brook School. The ladies and the pastor were given a home to live in on Sixth Street, which was amidst the homes of Hillburn's white families. I have no idea whether they paid for the property or whether it was given to them by the local powers that be. The family members resembled the colored people of Hillburn. They looked very much to be mixed with Native American blood, just as many of Hillburn's residents appeared. Miss Savory was considered the principal of the Brook School and taught the seventh and eighth grades. Cicely Gunner was the teacher for the kindergarten, which was held at the Brook Chapel. Mrs. Love worked in one of the area factories.

I recall that both Miss Roseboro and Miss Savory were good teachers but very strict. We learned the basic lessons like reading, social studies, and science, but we did not learn New York history. I guess it is because they were from the south and didn't know anything about our state. I really can't comment on how well they taught us because I have no way to compare, but I remember that all eighth grade students had to take the New York State Regents math exam (a statewide standardized test), and most in our school failed. All of the students had to take a second exam, even those who passed the first exam, because of the high failure rate.

A daily event at Brook School was physical education, which we called gym. We didn't have a playground, but at some point a set of monkey bars were installed next to our school for us to use. Most of the time we played stickball in the street in front of the school. When a car would pass by, the game would stop until it was safe to play again. On rare occasions, we would walk to the Hillburn firehouse, which was about a half-mile away on the white side of town, for indoor recreation. The white kids had a recreation teacher, but we did not have a gym teacher assigned to us. When we went to the firehouse, the teacher from the white school would lead us.

A white school nurse would visit our school from time to time, and a white music teacher, Miss Duvall, would also visit our school. She taught us songs like "Ol' Black Joe," "Possum Meat," and "Poor Old Ned." These are the words to "Poor Old Ned:"

> There was an old darkie
> His name was Uncle Ned.
> He died long ago, long ago.
> He had no wool on the top of his head
> In the place where the wool oughta to grow.
>
> Hang up the fiddle and the bow;
> Lay down the shovel and the hoe.
> There's no more work for poor old Ned.
> He's gone where the good darkies go!

As outrageous as the lyrics to the songs were, I really didn't notice that we were learning clearly racist songs. These were the songs that we were being taught to sing, and we learned them. As far as I knew, that's just what you did in music class. I don't even recall ever going home and telling my parents about what we were learning.

Shortly after the Andrews visit to Hillburn in 1931, the *Rockland Evening Journal*, a local newspaper, published a story about the NAACP reporting to Lt. Governor Herbert H. Lehman that the segregated Hillburn schools violated state law. The story ended by revealing that the Lt. Governor was a member of the NAACP Board of Directors and that the NAACP expected the Lt. Governor "to do all in his power to have the discrimination discontinued."[18]

Andrews wrote a supplemental memorandum regarding the Hillburn school system and he used the new document to memorialize some additional facts about the civil rights struggle. He noted that his investigation revealed that "the separate and distinct school for Negro children has existed at Hillburn for a long period of time—certainly before 1900."[19] He also wrote that "[school board president] Mr. Davidson frankly stated that it was the policy of the Board of Education to send all Negro pupils, from the first through the eighth grades in Hillburn, to the Brook School regardless of what section of the town they lived.[20]

As an interesting aside, Andrews had received an advance of $5.00 to help him make the 80-mile roundtrip between Hillburn and New York City. His itemized expense report indicates that his entire trip cost just $3.88, a very reasonable amount for the information he learned.

February 6, 1931

Expense in trip to Hillburn to
investigate school situation

Train fare to Hillburn.....$1.18
Fare to New Jersey   17
Train fare to New York   1.18
Lunch   .60
Dinner   .75
                       Total.$ 3.88

Advance by Nat'l Office $5.00
                         3.88
            Total..... $1.12

Itemized expense statement from NAACP Special
Legal Assistant William T. Andrews, 1931.

The New York lieutenant governor moved with dispatch and referred the Hillburn school matter to Frank P. Graves, the New York commissioner of education. Graves's deputy commissioner and legal counsel, Ernest Cole, wrote to Andrews within ten days of receiving the referral from the lieutenant governor, but his news was not what Andrews was expecting to hear. Cole wrote that New York education law had a provision for maintaining "separate schools for the instruction of colored children."[21] The letter went on to say that the constitutionality of the New York law had been upheld by the state's highest court on two occasions.[22] Undaunted, Andrews immediately wrote the deputy commissioner and pointed out to him that the law that was cited by the state had been repealed by the enactment of a new civil rights law in 1918 and asserted that "separate schools are against the policy of the state."[23]

Cole's rejoinder to Andrews disagreed with his assessment of the state of the civil rights law in New York. Cole explained that there was a distinction in the law between common school districts and union school districts and the laws banning separate schools for colored children applied only to union school districts.[24]

While the NAACP and the state of New York were sorting out the legal issues, my father was doing his own research concerning the segregated school system. He discovered that the white school was about to receive new books, and their used books were to be given to the colored school. This was an interesting development because Brook School did not have a library, and suddenly, after Mr. Andrews had visited our village, we were going to have books in our building. Pop also learned from his father-in-law (my grandfather), Samuel DeFreese Jr., that Mr. Davidson's father told someone that his wife had left $1,800 (presumably in her will) about ten years earlier to build a new colored school.[25] My father confirmed this fact with Thomas Dennison, the janitor at the colored school, but Mr. Dennison said that school officials claimed that they could not find any place in town to build a new school.[26]

Letter from Thomas Alexander to NAACP Special
Legal Assistant William T. Andrews. (1931)

By July of 1931, the NAACP had determined conclusively that the Hillburn schools violated civil rights laws. An internal memorandum from within the organization reveals that the situation was critical. A Mr. Pickens wrote to his colleague:

> There is no doubt that at Hillburn they have a jim crow school for the Colored children. The school is being neglected in all the ways in which jim crow schools are usually neglected. They even fail to put up signs to protect the children from fast driving motorists on the great highway (Route 17) that passes the school.

———

Mr. Alexander, officer of our Hillburn Branch, thinks he can make a bona fide case of complaint by some parents and patrons of the school in Hillburn. He has children in the school himself and, as a last resort, will be a complainant; although, it will be better if others will stand in the position of complainants since he must help to lead the fight for them.

It is said that there are six hundred colored people in Hillburn, and unfortunately most of them work for some large industrial concern and fear reprisals by this concern if they should be active and prominent in defense of their rights, especially in this school matter. This is a handicap. There are a few, however, who are willing to fight, and some are in a position to do the fighting. I suggested publically to the others that if they cannot engage in the fight, they can pay memberships and money for backing up the fight.

Mr. Alexander works in the Post Office in New York, which, perhaps, gives him impunity against successful attack by Hillburn white people. The Colored teachers in the Jim crow schools can hardly be expected to take part in the fight. If they will be neutral and keep their mouths shut and not help the segregationists, it will be about all that we can hope for from them.[27]

By the end of 1931, the fight for equality had taken another unexpected turn. The school board called a special meeting for the purpose of asking the residents of school district to dissolve the common school district and form a union free school district, a move intended to circumvent the New York civil rights laws that prevented the segregated school system from operating. The citizens voted to change the school district to a union free district, and there was no change in the segregation that had plagued the Hillburn schools. The "separate but equal" treatment of minority school children would continue for many years, even after New York passed a law that eliminated segregated public schools in 1938.

Between 1931 and the early 1940s, progress on integrating the Hillburn school system was slow. I was in grammar school during that time, and I remember that life went on in our village just as if nothing was going on. There were no editorials in the newspaper or protests by the citizens. The men in the village continued to work in the foundries run by Mr. Pierson and Mr. Davidson, and the separate schools continued undaunted.

Relations between the races outside of school were also frozen in time. Whites and coloreds rarely spent time together. In fact, the only time I remember regularly being in the same place as whites was in our village park, called the Fountain, during the winter months. There was a pond in the center of the park, and many residents would go ice-skating there. Even at the Fountain, however, the races didn't mix; we all skated on the same pond but stayed within our racial groups. A few of the white kids were friendly to my friends and me, particularly the Sovak, Wanamaker, and Long children, but we never played together.

The apparent quiet notwithstanding, the NAACP was still hard at work behind the scenes, trying to seek justice for the colored children of Hillburn. Everything came to a head, however, in 1943. As an editorial in the NAACP magazine, *The Crisis*, explained:

> Here was literally a feudal village, tucked away a scant hour from Manhattan. It maintained the last and only "Negro" school in the state. Its white people patronized the little colony of Negroes in the best ante-bellum tradition. They were "kind" to them. They "gave" them work. They "let" them live in a hollow on the other side of the highway. Years ago, they "set up" the Negro Brook school, a two-room shack, and later added two more rooms, the whole with outside toilets.
>
> But the Hillburn Negroes of 1943 are not the Negroes of 1913 or of 1903. They knew that the world had changed and they were tired of living in the past. So they announced they would not send their children to the dilapidated Brook school. The

result, after an interval in skirmishing, was that the
school was ordered closed.[28]

There was much more to the story than parents suddenly deciding
not to send their children to the colored school. In the period between
1931 and 1945, World War II erupted in Europe, and many Hillburn
residents, white and colored, fought in the war to protect the free-
doms upon which the United States had been founded. The war was a
reminder of the important role of colored families in American history.
We mattered as much as the whites.

Closer to home, Hillburn's colored families were enjoying more
economic security in the thirties and forties, in part because the war
effort created more job opportunities. In fact, women of color were
working at W. W. Snow's mammoth brake-shoe plant in Mahwah,
New Jersey, earning decent wages. Prior to the war, no colored people
were working at the plant. People were much less worried about losing
their sources of income if they spoke up about the segregated schools
because they were so badly needed in the workplace.

Also, the climate for civil rights advances had changed throughout
the country. New Yorkers of African descent grew more militant and
pushed for greater rights, including educational rights, and "alliances
with New Dealers, leftists, and religious activists—began pushing for
civil rights legislation, including a 1938 state law that officially forbade
racially separate schools in the state."[29]

By 1943, my father had stepped down as president of the Hillburn
chapter of the NAACP; that role now belonged to Marion Van Dunk
and a new group of village leaders. Ironically, some of the very people
who called him troublemaker were now spearheading the new charge
for equal rights for the Hillburn colored children. Pop was never one to
stand in the spotlight, but the new push for equality surely made him
proud, even if he was now watching from the sidelines.

Mrs. Van Dunk and the rest of the Hillburn NAACP board
members contacted a young lawyer who had been working with the
national NAACP to help integrate schools nationwide. That lawyer
was Thurgood Marshall. Marshall promised the Hillburn parents that
the NAACP would "back the local group to the limit to fight against
segregation."[30]

Thurgood Marshall was an up-and-coming attorney, who spent much of the 1930s and 1940s litigating civil rights cases that collectively led to the *Brown v. Board of Education* decision.[31] He successfully challenged the South's white primaries, overturned racially restrictive covenants, and had twenty-nine victories before the United States Supreme Court. Also, during that time, he assisted the colored parents in Hillburn.[32]

NAACP Attorney Thurgood Marshall is photographed with some of the parents of the Hillburn colored children. (circa 1943) The photo is courtesy of Library of Congress, Prints & Photographs Division, Visual Materials from the NAACP Records [reproduction number LC-USZ62-95524]

At the start of the 1943–1944 school year, Hillburn's colored families were fired up and ready to fight for integration. With help from Attorney Marshall, the parents planned a general strike; they would keep their children out of Brook School until the school district integrated the system. The wagons were circling around the school board because it had to submit a formal response to the charge that it was maintaining a segregated school system. The board really had no acceptable response because the school boundary it drew was Route 17, which was logical and which allowed a few colored children who lived on the white side of town to attend the white school. Where it made a mistake was to gerrymander the school boundaries to cross Route 17 to include the one white family that lived on the colored side of town.[33]

The Hillburn school desegregation effort was fairly widely known, at least within civil rights circles. The struggle in Hillburn was not the only northern town attempting to integrate its schools. In New York's Hudson Valley, similar battles were also taking place in Goshen (in Orange County to the northwest) and in New Rochelle (in Westchester County to the east). African American newspapers also spread the word, and the Hillburn integration effort was quickly connected to the national movement to integrate the United States and communities such as Berwyn, Pennsylvania; East Orange, New Jersey; and Springfield, Ohio.[34] Countee Cullen, a poet who rose to prominence in the Harlem Renaissance, even penned a poem about the struggles in my village. Titled, "Hillburn—The Fair," the piece was published in *The People's Voice* in New York City on October 30, 1943. It reads:

> Hillburn—The Fair
>
> God have pity
> On such a city
> Where parent teaches child to hate;
> God looks down
> On such a town
> Where Prejudice the Great
> Rules drunkenly
> And evilly
> What should be Liberty's estate.[35]

For decades after the integration of the white school, Hillburn residents have reminisced about the day that Thurgood Marshall padlocked the front doors of the white school. I don't remember the specific event, but I have heard the story from dozens of relatives and friends. Marshall is reported to have said that "if the colored children can't attend the Hillburn Main School, no children will attend," and he padlocked the school's front door.

Regardless of whether Marshall padlocked the school entrance, written history does tell us that Marshall tried to enroll five-year-old Allen Morgan Jr., a colored kid who had started at Brook School, knowing that he would be denied entry. The skilled attorney needed to take that step in order to have a basis to file a lawsuit against the school district.[36] I don't think Allen was chosen for a specific reason; he was a quiet kid. I think Marshall tried to enroll him because his mother consented. Of course, the school board denied Marshall's request to enroll Allen Morgan.

I was in high school at the time of Marshall's confrontation with the school board, and the happenings at the elementary school really didn't interest me that much. I knew there was controversy, but I don't recall the particulars. That was not the case throughout the village, however. Mr. Davidson, the school board president and one of the Hillburn pillars, reacted negatively to the news of the protest. He called it a celebrity stunt, and Mayor Creelman expressed his shock by blurting out that "all a Negro wants is a full belly."[37]

Hillburn suddenly was in the spotlight. We were no longer just the sleepy little village in the Ramapo Mountains. The NAACP magazine, *The Crisis*, covered our desegregation efforts extensively, and newspapers throughout the country picked up the story.[38] In addition, several notable Rockland County residents signed a petition in support of the striking families, including composer Kurt Weill, playwright Maxwell Anderson, and actress Helen Hayes.[39]

Historians report that, by October of 1943, "more than twenty thousand posters appeared on telephone poles and in bars, stores, and churches throughout Harlem (in New York City) advertising a 'mass rally' on behalf of the Hillburn boycott.... By mid-October, the protests and the threat of litigation bore fruit. In response to the NAACP's complaint, the state commissioner of education overruled the district's policy of segregation, shut down the Brook School, and ordered the enrollment of black students at Main (School)."[40]

CHAPTER 4

THE INTEGRATED SCHOOL

Once the colored children were able to attend the white school, the white parents immediately began to find other options for their kids. African American Hillburn resident, Dr. Travis Jackson, recalled that, once he started at the Hillburn Main School, there was only one white family that sent their children to the school.[41] That's because many of the white parents had removed their children and had enrolled them in area private schools. The *New York Age*, an influential African American newspaper that published stories from 1887 to 1953, reported that several white families sent their children to the catholic school in Suffern, and many enrolled their children in the Suffern Boys' School, a private school accredited by the state of New York.[42] The paper also reported that several families were sending their children to the public school in nearby Tuxedo, New York, which would have required the families to pay tuition because Tuxedo was in another county. [43]

All of the alternatives to attending the Hillburn Main School required families to pay tuition. This mass exodus to other schools was controversial, in part because most Hillburn families, regardless of race, were either working class or working poor and could not have paid the tuition at private schools. The prevailing thought in town was that a prominent part-time Hillburn resident was the source of the tuition funding.[44] In time, the white children returned to the school, and Hillburn School was finally integrated.

The integration of the school system was national news. Several newspapers carried the story, but the *Pittsburgh Courier* summed it up best:

Hillburn Parents Win

The lowly folk in the Ramapo Hills of New York State have won a magnificent battle.

They have smashed jim crowism, caused their jim crow school to be closed and forced their admittance to the school attended by ALL the children of Hillburn.

They did not have much education, and probably none in the town could boast of a Bachelor of Arts degree.

They are poor folk, living simply, scarcely making ends meet; but they are also old American stock—Negro, Indian, German and English—stemming from Revolutionary times, and very stubborn about what they think is right.

They decided that a jim crow school was not right and they refused to send their children there any more, even withstanding threats of jail.

How much farther would we be along the road of progress if the Negroes in every community showed the spirit of the "little people" of Hillburn, N.Y.?[45]

Integration of the Hillburn school system was just one step in the long journey to racial equality in the United States. In 1945, I graduated from Suffern High School, which, unlike the grammar schools in Hillburn, had always been integrated. Upon graduation, I enlisted in the navy and shipped off to see the world. During my years in the military, I was personally reminded of how complicated the racial struggle was in America. Despite serving my country, I was regularly discriminated against—even when traveling in uniform. Our ship would dock in Norfolk, Virginia, and I would typically take a train to get home to New York. Even though I had bonded with my shipmates while at sea, I was unable to travel with them for I was relegated to the colored car at the back of the train. Once, while hitchhiking home, I got a ride from a guy and his buddy in Washington, DC, who decided to stop at a road-side inn in Delaware for a bite. I explained to them that I didn't think I could eat in the establishment, but they insisted that we eat. The other guys ordered, but when I tried to do the same, the waitress told me that I had to go around to the back of the inn to get my food. The driver, surprised and outraged by this treatment, cancelled his order, and we drove on to New York without any further meal stops.

Leonard "Pete" Alexander in his navy uniform.
(1947) [Photo courtesy of Leonard Alexander]

Fast-forward to the fall of 1963, when it was time for my wife and me to enroll our oldest son in school. I had lived in Hillburn my entire life and probably never thought that one day I would have a child in the white school. That day did arrive, and two years later, our second son was enrolled in the same school. Their childhoods were very different from my own. Their classrooms were fully integrated and so were their circles of friends.

EPILOGUE

In 1983, my father died in my home in Middletown, New York, at the grand old age of ninety-five. He had lived a remarkable life, but the most remarkable part of that life may have been that he lived long enough to see two of his grandsons, my sons, Peter and Paul, attend Hillburn School—the white school—and to see one of my maternal cousins, Mildred DeGroat, teach third grade in that school.

Our family knew that Pop had played some part in the integration of the Hillburn School, but we really didn't appreciate how significant a role he had played until we received word from the Rockland County (New York) Office of the County Executive that my father, Thomas Ulysses Alexander, had been selected for 2012 induction into the Rockland County Civil/Human Rights Hall of Fame. He shared that honor with Thurgood Marshall, who had been inducted just seven years earlier. On Friday, March 8, 2013, I attended a ceremony in Stony Point, New York, along with some of my nieces and nephews, and we were honored to witness the celebration of my father's contributions to the advancement of civil rights in education in Hillburn. I was presented with certificates from township of Clarkstown supervisor Alexander Gromack; Harriet Cornell, chairwoman of the Rockland County Legislature; Assemblywoman Elien Jaffee; New York State senator David Carlucci; and Congresswoman Nita Lowey. It was a very special day for our family.

Those attending the event received a written program, in which there was a tribute to each Hall of Fame inductee. Dr. Travis Jackson wrote the tribute to Pop. Travie, as we called him, was an excellent choice. He was a few years behind me in school, and because of the Hillburn desegregation effort, he was able to attend the white school. Travie not only went on to college, he also earned graduate degrees and served as an educator in the Ramapo School District and later as an administrator in the Ridgewood, New Jersey, public schools. He too was an inductee into the Rockland County Civil/Human Rights Hall of Fame in 2004.

He wrote the following:

> In the decade between 1930 and 1940, the Village of Hillburn, very little progress was made regarding race relations. Life was orderly, and relations between the races were positive just so long as the people of color did not overstep their bounds. Often it takes only one person, who was free from any reprisals against his activism. Such a man was Thomas Ulysses Alexander.[46]

I suspect that my father would have been a bit uncomfortable with all of the attention that was generated by his induction into the county's Hall of Fame. He would have considered his part in this important history lesson as simply one man doing what was right. I know, however, that the attention was very important to the residents of Hillburn and to ensuring that the historical record of segregation and integration of the Hillburn school system is accurately reported for future generations.

Thanks, Pop!

This is a monument on the grounds of the former
Hillburn School and it memorializes Thurgood Marshall's
contributions to integrating the Hillburn school system.
(2014) Mary Galindez Short, photographer.

NOTES

(Endnotes)

1   Julienne Marshall, "Hillburn named for its stream," *The Journal News*, p. 9 (Feb. 19, 2003).
2   Julienne Marshall (note 1).
3   Village of Hillburn Centennial Celebration program (July 24, 1993).
4   Business Review, Spring 1974 (Special Edition).
5   The Home and Store News, "The Highways of the Revolution," by Gardner F. Watts (March 28, 1973).
6   Business Review (note 1), p. 3.
7   Business Review (note 1), p. 3.
8   Business Review (note 1), p. 3.
9   "Recollections of Local History by Readers of the Home and Store News," p. 1.
10 The Cornell Alumni News, Vol. 23, p. 63.
11 Letter from Irwin Esmond to William T. Andrews, August 5, 1930.
12 Letter from Thomas U. Alexander to William T. Andres, September 6, 1930.

13   Report on Visit to Hillburn, William T. Andrews, February 2, 1931.

14   Ibid. at p. 3.

15   Ibid.

16   Ibid. at p. 5

17   Ibid.

18   *NAACP Reports to Lieut. Gov. Lehman, Segregated School at Hillburn*, Rockland Evening Journal, February 6, 1931.

19   Memorandum in re Separate Schools, Hillburn, New York, by William T. Andrews, February 4, 1931.

20   Ibid at p. 2.

21   Letter from Ernest E. Cole to William T. Andrews, February 13, 1931, citing Article 36 of the New York Education Law, sec. 921.

22   Ibid.

23   Letter from William T. Andrews to Ernest E. Cole, February 16, 1931.

24   Letter from Ernest E. Cole to William T. Andrews, February 24, 1931.

25   Postcard from Thomas U. Alexander to William T. Andrews, February 27, 1931.

26   Ibid.

27   Memorandum from Mr. Pickens to Mr. White, July 14, 1931.

28   The Crisis, Nov. 1943, Vol. 50, no. 11, pp. 327, 344.

29   Fog of War: The Second World War and the Civil Rights Movement, Kevin M. Kruse and ed. Stephen Tuck, 95, (2012).

30   Thomas J. Sugrue, Sweet Land of Liberty: The Forgotten Struggle for Civil Rights in the North, 166 (Random House 2008).

31   American Legends: The Life of Thurgood Marshall, Charles River Editors, ISBN 978149224318.

32   Ibid.

33   Ibid. at p. 165.

34   Fog of War (Kruse and Tuck 2012) at p. 96.

35   Countee Cullen Collected Poems, ed. Major Jackson 264 (American Poets Project 2013).

36   Fog of War (Kruse and Tuck 2012) at p. 87.

37   Sugrue at 167.

38 Ibid.

39 Ibid.

40 Ibid at p. 168.

41 Bill Batson, Nyack Sketch Log: Hillburn Case Precursor of *Brown v. Board of Education*, Nyack News & Views, May 16, 2014, available at http://www.nyacknewsandviews.com/2014/05/nsl-hillburn.

42 The New York Age, "White Pupils Quit Main Hillburn School After Negroes Are Ordered Admitted; Go to Private School," p. 1 (October 23, 1943).

43 Ibid.

44 Frank Marshall Davis, Writings of Frank Marshall Davis: A Voice of the Black Press (John Edgar Tidwell ed.) 107 (Univ. Press of Mississippi 2007).

45 The Pittsburgh Courier, "Hillburn Parents Win," p. 6 (October 23, 1943).

46 Reception Program, Rockland County Commission on Human Rights, March 8, 2013, p. 4.

ABOUT THE AUTHORS

LEONARD "PETE" ALEXANDER was the fifth of seven children born to Thomas and Sara Alexander. Six boys and one girl. They lived in the western area of the village of Hillburn, NY. If you weren't of the "white race," that was where you lived. They had their own church, referred to originally as Brook Chapel and later became Brook Presbyterian Church. This church was the modern replacement, in 1893, of the mountain chapel of which his great-grand father was the preacher.

They, "people of color" attended the segregated school, "Brook School," in Hillburn, NY. Interestingly, when his mother attended school in Hillburn, there was only one school; that school was integrated. As a student, he would rate himself as "average," as far as the boys were rated. Leonard's weakest phase of school was reading. He was more interested in mechanics and construction.

After graduating from high school, Leonard enlisted in the U.S. Navy where he worked as a repairperson. After he left the Service, he worked in construction for about 10 years. His father suggested that he apply for a job in the Postal Service. Leonard's father worked in the New York City General Post Office. He had tried for a transfer up to a post office in Rockland County, where Hillburn is located. He never did get a transfer. In about 1968, a large Postal Concentration Center was built in Rockland County. They were hiring transfers from NYC post offices, but they were not hiring people-of-color. One of his relatives, who was a veteran of World War II, applied for a job there but he was not hired. He happened to work for a prominent person in Rockland County. That person knew the person in charge of the hiring at that facility and he was directly responsible for about a dozen people- of- color being hired at that facility. Leonard's father knew of only three people of color, who worked at a post office in Rockland County. He ultimately got hired and, once they were working in the concentration center, most people who worked there treated them in a friendly way. He dares say that most of the people-of-color worked more diligently than many of the others.

After retiring from the Postal Service, at the age of 60 years old, his wife and he moved from New York to Champaign, Illinois and operated a travel agency for many years. They have been there since 1989. They are now 86 years old. What else could they ask for?

———⁓⁓ഛ⁓⁓———

PETER C. ALEXANDER grew up in Hillburn, New York and attended Suffern High School in a neighboring town, just like is father. In 1976, he left New York to attend Southern Illinois University in Carbondale, Illinois and never returned to his suburban New York City home.

Peter earned a Bachelor's Degree in Political Science from SIU and then attended law school at Northeastern University in Boston. He served as a law clerk in the U.S. District Court and the U.S. Bankruptcy Court for the Central District of Illinois and then practiced law in central Illinois for seven years. His practice was focused on bankruptcy law and civil and criminal litigation in federal court.

In 1992, Peter left practice to become a law professor at The Dickinson School of Law in Carlisle, Pennsylvania. Dickinson subsequently merged with the Pennsylvania State University and served the merged institutions as Associate Dean for Research and Faculty Development. In 2003, he left Penn State Dickinson to become the Dean at Southern Illinois University School of Law. He served in that capacity for six years and then returned to the faculty. In 2011, he was named the Founding Dean of Indiana Tech Law School in Fort Wayne.

In 2014, Peter stepped down as Dean at Indiana Tech and currently spends time writing and lecturing on topics as diverse as bankruptcy, legal education, financial literacy, and civil rights.

CPSIA information can be obtained at www.ICGtesting.com
Printed in the USA
LVOW08s1040200715

446862LV00001B/18/P